The Polymers

The Polymers

Adam Dickinson

ANANSI

This edition published in 2013 by
House of Anansi Press Inc.
110 Spadina Avenue, Suite 801
Toronto, ON, M5V 2K4
Tel. 416-363-4343
Fax 416-363-1017
www.houseofanansi.com

Distributed in Canada by
HarperCollins Canada Ltd.
1995 Markham Road
Scarborough, ON, M1B 5M8
Toll free tel. 1-800-387-0117

Distributed in the United States by
Publishers Group West
1700 Fourth Street
Berkeley, CA, 94710
Toll free tel. 1-800-788-3123

House of Anansi Press is committed to protecting our natural environment.
As part of our efforts, the interior of this book is printed on paper made from
second-growth forests and is acid-free.

17 16 15 14 13   1 2 3 4 5

Library and Archives Canada Cataloguing in Publication

Dickinson, Adam, 1974-
The polymers / Adam Dickinson.

Issued also in electronic format.
ISBN 978-1-77089-217-0 (pbk).—ISBN 978-1-77089-349-8 (bound.)

I. Title.
PS8557.I3235P65 2013   C811'.6   C2012-906722-9

Library of Congress Control Number: 2012950665

Cover design: Brian Morgan
Text design and typesetting: Alysia Shewchuk

Canada Council   Conseil des Arts   ONTARIO ARTS COUNCIL
for the Arts   du Canada   CONSEIL DES ARTS DE L'ONTARIO

We acknowledge for their financial support of our publishing program
the Canada Council for the Arts, the Ontario Arts Council, and the Government of Canada
through the Canada Book Fund.

Printed and bound in Canada

*for Erin
and Millicent,
my macromolecules*

In the hierarchy of the major poetic substances, it figures as a disgraced material... It is a 'shaped' substance: whatever its final state, plastic keeps a flocculent appearance, something opaque, creamy and curdled, something powerless ever to achieve the triumphant smoothness of Nature.

Roland Barthes, "Plastic," from *Mythologies*

Polymers are giant molecules composed of numerous repeating parts. As long chains, they form the basis of both synthetic and natural plastics—the structures of the human brain, skin, hair, as well as DNA are all composed of polymers. As prevalent as polymers are biologically, plastic, as a cultural and industrial commodity, is similarly omnipresent. Its ubiquity, however, marks a curious contradictory tension: plastic is at once outmoded and futuristic, colloquial and scientific, a polluting substance that is also intimately associated with our lives. The origins of plastic, as an industrial material, have extended and continue to extend out of attempts to mimic or substitute for things in the natural world. Therefore, plastic marks both the presence and the absence of natural objects, embodying tension between the literal and the metaphorical, as it recreates the world as an alternate or translated reality.

Plastic is an emergent expression of the petrochemical age. Its pervasiveness, as a tool and as physical and chemical pollution, makes it an organizing principle (a poetics) for recurring forms of language, for obsessive conduct, and for the macromolecular arrangements of people and waste in geopolitical space. This book directs its attention to sequencing the seven principal synthetic resins that predominate in Western petroleum culture. If DNA is the digital memory of a species passed forward through time, then the social polymers of iterative behaviour, including their flammable appendices and polluting precipitates, constitute a plastic shovel with which the analogue body digs its own grave. Or plants its flag on the moon. Or builds a bionic limb. Plastic is the grinning salt of capitalism, Karl Marx said in speculative writings on the hydrocarbon economy. What follows is a closer look at the teeth

Plastic is an emergent expression of the petrochemical age. Its pervasiveness, as a tool and as physical and chemical pollution, makes it an organizing principle (a poetics) for recurring forms of language, for obsessive conduct, and for the macromolecular arrangements of people and waste in geopolitical space. This book directs its attention to sequencing the seven principal synthetic resins that predominate in Western petroleum culture. If DNA is the digital memory of a species passed forward through time, then the social polymers of iterative behaviour, including their flammable appendices and polluting precipitates, constitute a plastic shovel with which the analogue body digs its own grave. Or plants its flag on the moon. Or builds a bionic limb. Plastic is the grinning salt of capitalism, Karl Marx said in speculative writings on the hydrocarbon economy. What follows is a closer look at the teeth

PETE

A polymer is the imperial dream of parades. Humans are creatures of habit and pandemic. Information is a competitively stressed disorder.

HDPE

A polymer is the largest idea to survive serious thinking. Analyses make matrices of Procrustean mattresses, make jams jarred in aromatic rings of amnion.

V

A polymer is a staircase to the second floor of a house built by Escher. Helical planks carry one side of the family to the next with acidic delinquency.

LDPE

A polymer is the parallax in pretending. Duplicitous hams butterfly fibs to milquetoast cling-wraps in the all-night greasy spoons.

PP

A polymer is the flashback occasioned by fragrance. Artificial flowers bouquet the centrepiece with hospital wards and wet raincoats.

PS

A polymer is the linguistic mycelium of plastic, the path of the translator into the misread monkey bars of pituitary piracy.

OTHER

We have nothing to read but our chains. Our chains reread us precipitously.

1. Polyester

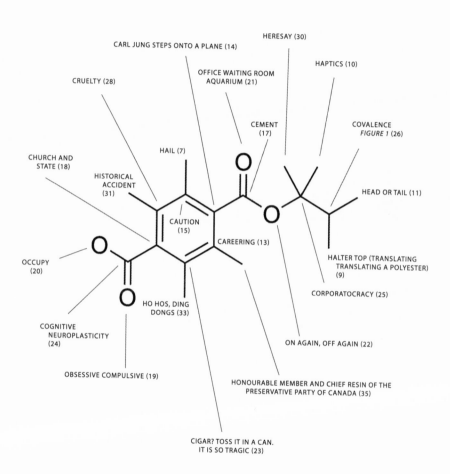

CARL JUNG STEPS ONTO A PLANE (14)

HERESAY (30)

OFFICE WAITING ROOM AQUARIUM (21)

HAPTICS (10)

CRUELTY (28)

CEMENT (17)

COVALENCE
FIGURE 1 (26)

CHURCH AND STATE (18)

HAIL (7)

HISTORICAL ACCIDENT (31)

HEAD OR TAIL (11)

CAUTION (15)

CAREERING (13)

OCCUPY (20)

HALTER TOP (TRANSLATING TRANSLATING A POLYESTER) (9)

CORPORATOCRACY (25)

HO HOS, DING DONGS (33)

COGNITIVE NEUROPLASTICITY (24)

ON AGAIN, OFF AGAIN (22)

OBSESSIVE COMPULSIVE (19)

HONOURABLE MEMBER AND CHIEF RESIN OF THE PRESERVATIVE PARTY OF CANADA (35)

CIGAR? TOSS IT IN A CAN. IT IS SO TRAGIC (23)

Polyethylene terephthalate, $C_{10}H_8O_4$

Hello from inside
the albatross
with a windproof lighter
and Japanese police tape.
Hello from staghorn
coral beds
waving at the beaked whale's
mistake,
all six square metres
of fertilizer bags.
Hello from can-opened
delta gators,
taxidermied
with twenty-five grocery sacks
and a Halloween Hulk mask.
Hello from the zipped-up
leatherback
who shat bits of rope for a month.
Hello from bacteria
making their germinal way
to the poles in the pockets
of packing foam.
Hello from low-density
polyethylene dropstones
glacially tilled
by desiccated,
bowel-obstructed camels.
Hello from six-pack rings
and chokeholds,
from breast milk

and cord blood,
from microfibres
rinsed through yoga pants
and polyester fleece,
biomagnifying predators
strafing the treatment plants.
Hello from acrylics
in G.I. Joe.
Hello from washed up
fishnet thigh-highs
and frog suits
and egg cups
and sperm.
Hello.

HALTER TOP (TRANSLATING TRANSLATING A POLYESTER)

Polyethylene terephthalate

Let the python plot the thorn.
Let the hornet paper the tree.
Let pollen apron the path to the pharaoh.

Neoprene phyla are really an alloy art.
The telltale pattern,
the protean trophy pelt.

Nylon antelope threaten the Tylenol people,
open the paternal peephole to the athlete panther
and her alternate entropy.

Her teeth apply to the planetary apathy.
They are polar, they are throttle,
the error apparent

to the hyperreal
apple.

Inspired by cigarettes, folding chairs, and the flourished gestures that accompany escalating disagreements, Plasticus Corporation (a subsidiary of Dow Chemical) quietly moved into researching the biological effects of touch on memory. The idea was to engineer nostalgia into the flexible surfaces of goods. Take, for example, the proleptic goodbye of an ice cube tray, the Merry Christmas grip of a Swiss Army knife, or the complementary blisters bevelled by borrowed cash. Researchers impregnated experimental plastics with erotic, platonic, and ritualistic dispersants in order to approximate the uncanny and its unguent penetration into the rehearsals of the brain's transcriptional grease. Soon, the golden age of mothers was upon us. Wine pairings were devised. Moods were adjusted. People saw their fingerprints blinking everywhere like biometric avalanche beacons. In the midst of the frenzy, in bathrooms where blow-dryers whipped pierced barley ears into Arcadian compost, in soliloquies sprung to life on the pocket-dialed sidewalks down memory lane, in gear-boxed convertibles retrograding the open road, in Archimedean armchairs armed with bygone gamepads, in the protopathic nuzzling of machined memorabilia, the retraction went unnoticed. Plasticus had forged the data. All the handheld déjà-vus made it feel like a publicity stunt. The hoax was taken for a hoax and the polyester lilies went on feeling up the valley.

HEAD OR TAIL

The message is fireworks
from a few streets over,

digitally remastered
by cherry bomb squads for whom

the message is roman candles
making blood meals

in a dog's stare
through the Christmas lights

of a bad dream, during which
the message is a broken bottle

rocket in a wireless head
evacuating directions

to unmarked urinary proteins as
the message brakes

for motorcycle surf and Catherine wheels,
putting a stop to digestion, reading

out the riot act in cortisol
and adrenaline where stereoisomers

open cans of animal fat
with skeleton keys to find

the message that some of us will pant
or cry nonstop

while others will begin
to shut down completely.

CAREERING

After the introduction
                    of polyurethane
the unexpected comebacks
                    collapsed and today
only a few minor accolades
                    still fatten figurines escaped
from commemorative bowls
                    championed by pressure-
sensitive graduates performing
                    the lipophilic ends of somersaults
in matriculating sieves
                    to lick moisture
off the inside of merit
                    where it's difficult
to hear clearly
                    through the dufflebagged lisp
of expanding memory foam
                    for any change in fortune
or the opportunity to see
                    you again Mrs. Robinson

Lunch boxes and lipstick
are our mothers.
We live in formative melodies
composed by the organs
it takes to be awakened
to emollients and parabens.
As great as the meaning of fertilizer
to our victory over the animals,
so great is also its meaning
for a motif of flight risk.
We watch the air-conditioner
fight the escalator
as a rite of passage in the arbitrary
arboretum of the shopping mall.
Food courts organize appetites
for deforestations weeping with shelf lives.
The cost of building a bridge
to the physical world
is vinyl siding
and butcher paper inclined to a life
of unidentifiable juice.
Archetypes fatten
until the fleshy parts are autopilots
reuniting red-eyes with runways
and kept-up appearances.
It'll always be easier to culture mediums
than to think autonomous
products of the unconscious.
The wind informs the wing
and the coffee mug the hand.
Goodbye and thank you for having me.

CAUTION

Danger, you have cursed the bridge

Falling shoulders may obscure the ice

Risk of drawing

It is indirection to smoke in here

Please return all hands to the supervision of transport

Citations are necessary frost, then submit for apparel

Actual weight may not have a figure

Form requires incline

Unpaid shudders, loose gravel

Cardholder ices first, then credit

Open wounds in the water

Before sounding your arm, return to the city position

The traditional belts, areas east of the lakes

Accumulations in the overnight towers

And the charity of your writing

Point form is the body of rush

Do not induce homilies

Consult a metaphysician

The ground connects everywhere

CEMENT

The objective for affected neighbourhoods is to rethink the tooth. Creep or permanent deformation may be experienced by casting gold alloys, by playing parts of inflammations, where early clinical failure has resulted in the demise and relocation of clinics. The Staples Thesis of economic development must be discarded save for the influence of the beaver. The biological response to plaque is always poor, so the result is a loss of translucency and surface crazing, a lack of adequate mechanical properties and inner-city parks. At first in small increments, but later on a wider scale, the composite can be injected into prepared cavities. Derelict assemblies, minimum wage, broken fire escapes, these are the osteological links for which full crowns or even bridges can be built. Make methods out of lips, make coupling agents out of chemical and photo initiation. Always transport individuals in saline, milk, or another willing mouth. After six months at the temperature of a tongue, creep decreases. Note that the low creep-values of saturated solutions polarize the relief of stresses between faces.

Are you going to Dracula or Frankenstein? This one's six bucks.

Let's just go eat, it's hot. Vous autres, vous arrivez juste du McDo?

You changed mine without asking. As a person, right? It should be

coming soon, but I like to think of having a normal smile. There's

two there and he's got the other three. You can just go straight ahead,

actually. The girl over there, comme ça, and said to me alright for both.

The haunted one's mine. Il faut checké la grandeur des enfants—les

Ontariens, tabarnak! Sylvain, t'as payé avec ta carte? Mais non! Just

push to the end. C'est quoi l'problème là? After this we should do

something together. Oh, you're not plugged in. You have to hold onto

the handles. I feel crappy most of the time, but the flash is on. Daddy?

make a roof for the people, and the people walk
down the street with resin for a roof, and the roof
has magnesium in it, and sulphur, and the people
walk down the street with resin in their hair, and
resins are always falling from the sky to the ground,
and the birds make a people in the sky, a people
of the resin, and the resin is composed of sky, and
it composes the sky, and the people walking down
the street are the strings of resins, and covering
their hair with their arms, with newspapers, with
umbrellas, the people are the birds of resins throwing
their landings in the air like people for whom landings
are uncommon, like people committed to the ex-
pulsion of landings, the resins coming down upon
them like people driven out of countries discovered
by resins or that have discovered resins in veins,
in the countertops of suburbs, and people walk
down the street with resins for hair, with countries
committed to colour, with the bonds between them
the birds circling, and people walking down the street
with hunched shoulders so as not to look up and
call the resins by name, call the resins in the name
of the birds, the people, circling and loosening

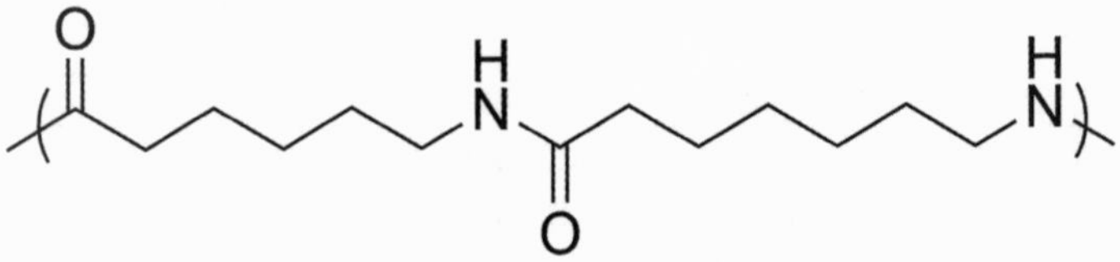
O
H
N
H
N
O

OFFICE WAITING ROOM AQUARIUM

We have to wait.

We have to wait to get fixed.

There's no cartoons.

We have to wait right here.

There's a fish tank here.

There's not many fishes.

There's a couple of fishes.

He has to wait.

He has a booboo.

Is it a big booboo?

I don't know, Cynthia.

He has to wait.

Where do Smarties live?

Taking care of things, Sweetie.

Paris is quiet and the good citizens are happy. Dandelion heads have dried to polyhedral fireworks in the gardens. Their dandruff riots wait for wind and fresh hair. Organ donors fix pipedreams preoccupied with the overlooked contribution of the gall bladder to modern telepathy. Mosquitoes pass along malaria like constructive criticism, while the buzz on the street is run-on sentences accruing in prisons with dangled modifiers and infinitives split along party lines. Business incubators disperse their eggs on the fabric of passing interests. Through word of mouth, body languages continue to thrive and hairstyles pile up in dangerous neighbourhoods like Braille infographics for social invisibility. Under stress, pathogens sense quorum in the fumbling expressions of survivor guilt. Recalling the aperiodic fables of pragmatic misunderstandings, turf wars repeat themselves in microwaveable webs. *Let your communication be, Yea, yea; Nay, nay: for whatsoever is more than these cometh of evil.*

For all intensive purposes, the fire distinguishers
are pigments of the imagination. Unparalyzed
in the history of this great country, our enemies
are holding us hostile. It bottles the mind to think
that we take for granite the apples and organs
hanging on tender hooks as a pose to bearing the blunt
of the escape goat gone awry with the crutch of the matter.
Needles to say, at the pentacle of patriarticle politics
we cannot phantom the depths to which
battering eyelids skewer the results to make ends meat.
We shutter to think that a seizure salad
made of fall foilage mine as well be one foul swoop
of poison ivory. In the same vain, we are in sink
with the insinnuendos and internally grateful
for the poultrygeist performing the Heineken remover
on a nation long stricken with the chicken pops.
It is perhaps a blessing in the skies that the hewn cries
sound like flaws in the ointment as we cease the day,
udderly disappointed by the ludicrust bowl in a china shop
and its new leash on life.

Humans are creatures of habit + pandemic
↳ p. 2

[new paths in the brain]

COGNITIVE NEUROPLASTICITY

Chancery Lane Station to Rolls Road — *are they close to each other?*

Leave on the left HIGH HOLBORN
Forward HOLBORN
Comply HOLBORN CIRCUS
Leave by ST. ANDREW STREET
Forward SHOE LANE
Left STONECUTTER STREET
Right FARRINGDON STREET
Forward LUDGATE CIRCUS
Forward NEW BRIDGE STREET
Forward UNILEVER JUNCTION
Forward BLACKFRIARS BRIDGE
Forward BLACKFRIARS ROAD
Left SOUTHWARK STREET
Right SOUTHWARK BRIDGE ROAD
Left MARSHALSEA ROAD
Forward LONG LANE
Bear right GREAT DOVER STREET
Comply BRICKLAYERS ARMS ROUNDABOUT
Leave by OLD KENT ROAD
Left ROWCROSS STREET

ROLLS ROAD on Left and Right

- takes a long + complicated path
- like a street detour, the brain rewires itself
- brain is like a polymer — made up of neurons (repeating units)
  ↳ example of natural polymer vs. synthetic
- we are creatures of habit → goes against this (neuroplasty).

↳ streets occupied by cars (monomers)
↳ countries made by streets.

24

Recent
discoveries
have identi-
fied a series of
resins respon-
sible for the accu-
mulation of un-
truths in the human
nose. *The bad faith, the*
bluff, and *the bareface* are
all semi-crystalline lattices
that repeat themselves in
networks of plausible solu-
tions. The result is stiff upper-
lipping on rhinoplastic surfaces.
In the case of *puffery*, the nasal mu-
cosa, under sworn interdigitation
and chronic compulsive behaviour,
leads to amassed consumer comestibles
and combustibles via peacock-pastried
testimonials. *Through the teeth*, exaggerated
omissions have cavitied balloting performanc-
es according to the false pretences of the view
from nowhere. Bolstered statistics congest the para-
nasal sinuses, forcing exclamatory inflammations and
leveraged haemorrhaging from olfactoried weapons
stiffened in polygraphic formations. Dissembling and
ignoble, the *white* lies just beneath the skin, where over
time it assumes the bailed-out interests of the greater good.

Found in small quantities
of combusted hydrocarbons
in the deep-spaced
recesses of fatigue,
this geodesic fullerene
produces the tethered filament
necessary for lifting
aromatic nano-dreams
into confectionary orbit.

Its adhesive properties,
expressed in jellybean parenting,
are mechanical
in the fashion of foot
and ball and ball
and spoon fed
polygons, abstracted
from the kitchen cosmonautics
of father-daughter cells
gelled in geosynchronous
gumdrops.

Space-walked
and sleepyheaded,
the orthogonal projections
make a ribcage
for the globular clusters of the most
exospheric dreamers.

CRUELTY

Bubble wrap fucks with us
like a rhyme scheme
of blistered ellipses.
Pointed fingers arrive daily

enveloped in the tender-buttoned
pneumatics of circular breathing.
In other spheres of influence,
convex candidates bloat

behind police barricades
while the housing slump
leaks everywhere
stinking of mackerel-economics.

A boy with aplastic anaemia
can be touched through mitts
sewn to the heart-attacked walls of his chamber.
The sound of the compressor

swim-bladders conversation.
Speech balloons distend in the illegible air
over sugar highs and glaciers
and ambulance chasers.

Setting aside the mustard
and ketchup argument
that citizens of non-rotating planets
fail to dream,

the scenery of our lives
blows by like vapour barrier.
To relieve stress,
we press the pressure until it populates.

- how polymers in our lives can be cruel
  ↳ police barricades = plastic
  ↳ economics = money = plastic
  ↳ a plastic anemia = natural - BMI error
  ↳ sugar = made of monomers (sucrose)
  ↳ glaciers = H₂0 molecules make ice crystal lattice

- the very polymers that make us up
also work against us.

Rumour has it the out-of-towners drove straight up through the *heart of Dixie*, then *north to the future*, to *the Grand Canyon* in its *natural state*. The *golden constitution* claims to be *the first* to *celebrate and discover sunshine*. All of this makes *a Pacific wonderland* of *aloha, peached* to *the famous potatoes* in their *amber waves of grain* and *big sky dairyland*. Given the *state of corn*, the *unbridled spirit* is a *sportsman's paradise* of *10,000 lakes* lost *in flight* over *wheat*, where *iodine* is the *empire of native America*. It's been said in the *land of Lincoln* that *you've got a friend* in *beef*. *The flute player* sounds good to me in *vacationland* while I *drive carefully* through *Great Lakes splendour* buoyed by *hospitality* that means *show-me-the silver* statutes already glistening in *enchanted gardens* of democratic *keystones*. The *greatest snow on earth* is a *wild and wonderful lone star* stating in full *colour*, before the *ocean*, the *green mountains*, and the *evergreens*, that the *great face* of the *birthplace of aviation lives free or dies*, while cars mate methodically in lots according to mudflapped theories illustrated with unrinsed plates.

HISTORICAL ACCIDENT

The problem with billiards was elephants.
The gentlemen felt the veldt
and its horn-rimmed hunters,

       commando side-pockets
       dressed in the misdirected carapace
       of vigilante cues, was too risky

              for the lamp-lit bowling green felt,
              its evenings of genteel smoke
              and designer holsters.

       The billiard ball makers
       baked a contest:
       imagine a rack without tusks,

a rock with no rust,
a rake from the comfort of chemistry
and slaves.

       With money on the rail
       they grew knife handles,
       candle wax, and combs.

              They grew false teeth,
              safety glass, and window curtains
              for armoured cars.

       Later, deep into a sore throat,
       someone dressed a wound with waterproof plaster
       and an emulsion for photographs

calling combination
ethyl to alcohol
to diethyl ether.

The contest blew apart
like unintentional english.
One account had balls hitting

and exploding into salvos
that caused cowboys
to draw their guns.

They took backhanded
bank shots on safari
through the tablelands

in the contraband complements
of clear-eyed bottles
and their hard, threaded caps.

The food pyramids

have been hacked.

Likewise the serving size

and its soap scum.

More and more tight pants

are now birdcalls

scaling wet-bulb temperatures

for mystified sugar.

What began

as an innocent hankering

for ambrosia salad

and decantered hooves

has become

a long chain of heists.

The pie fork

and the kidney

struggle in their second languages.

Each mouthful gets by

speaking nitrogen

and soft packaging.

He tried horn, shellac, rubber, and hair
He tried shrink-wrap, juice bottles, and Teflon
He tried rinsing and repeating
He tried ending with an "s" when referring to the matter
(any dropped letters were saved for the semi-solid adjective)
He tried paints, varnishes, and latex gloves
He tried lubricating additives for colour
He tried laminates and ministered abrasives
He tried to be flexible
(characteristics that come from a family of polyesters)
He tried umbrellas, cup holders, and rayon sweaters
He tried carefully machining sand
He tried bending his knees before lifting
He tried various shapes, either singly or together, under heat and pressure
    to get the chemistry right
He tried to sit in every seat to build a backbone of novelty cheques
    stretching oils to greases, greases to waxes, waxes to Tupperware,
    billiard balls, Kevlar, and hard hats
He tried to keep it moving, amorphous and crystalline, nylons running
    with leaks, acrylic accounting and covalent committees
    covertly dispersing available light, but it all became rigid
    at room temperature
He had no choice but to gum, melt, or craze it—his epoxy, his prosthesis:
    a Plexiglas house with his picture in every room
    melted and cooled, melted and cooled,
    made to fracture easily,
    predictably,
without effort

2, 4. POLYETHYLENE

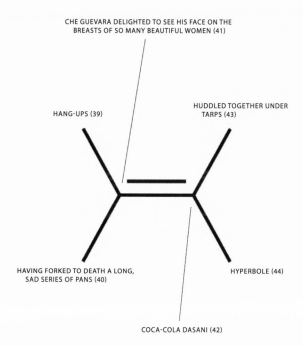

CHE GUEVARA DELIGHTED TO SEE HIS FACE ON THE
BREASTS OF SO MANY BEAUTIFUL WOMEN (41)

HANG-UPS (39)

HUDDLED TOGETHER UNDER
TARPS (43)

HAVING FORKED TO DEATH A LONG,
SAD SERIES OF PANS (40)

HYPERBOLE (44)

COCA-COLA DASANI (42)

C_2H_4

I hate my genitals.
They remind me of communism.
Who needs another vanguard party
ascending the staircase
à la mode?
Fish hang in chlorinated biphenyls
like unrequited high-fives.
I feel fat
just looking at their bleak schematics
for common ownership
and poor motility.
It's hard not to dwell
on equipment failures.
Fur hats get stained
with gravy trains and show trials
in all the unlaundered cornfields.
The problem
is my Bolshevik asshole,
my sick-building sensitivity
to the indignity of not degrading
in sunlight, or in soil,
or at the unpollinated end
of a spring break break-up.
Allergies are such a squeamish response to sex
and satellite states.
There's no use complaining,
the ombudspeople have already burst into leaf
and all the lines are bread.

Let's go.
Pack up the serviette flags,
what's left of the wine,
the tidal bore stains
and continental shelves
tipped with headaches
and hand grenades.
Let's leave
before they make us,
before the streets crowd
with miscarriages
and overheated oil,
greased by livestock
and their hung parliament
stomachs.
Loose-leaf every love letter
out of the stop bath,
dislocate the dog fur
from the leg-hold maps,
empty your pockets
of bird breath
and ventilation shafts.
Stainmaster the lawn
and break up the soap,
abandon your sex to a stump
of creaseless clothes.
Get the hell out,
let's go.

CHE GUEVARA DELIGHTED TO SEE HIS FACE ON THE
BREASTS OF SO MANY BEAUTIFUL WOMEN

a a a alps and applicable at at before best beverages bicarbonates bottle bottled calcium chlorides clean collection commerce composition content cool dissolved do dry exist fat facilities facts fluoride french from in ion limited magnesium mineral mineral neck nitrates not not nutrition of of of place potassium recyclable refill refund refund registered salts saturated see significant silica sodium source spring store sulphates the the trademark where where zero

HUDDLED TOGETHER UNDER TARPS

It turns out one need not
    study

the prevailing
    decorative trends

and aesthetic theories
    of the past

in order to understand
    what kind of architectural

styles were typical
    during some historical

period. All one needs
    is basic knowledge

of the mechanical
    properties, elasticity,

and strength
    of the building materials

used
    at the time.

It was simple, really.
She was in love with riptides
and couldn't go back.
He had insulted her dolphin kick
and dog paddled the length
of a vodka punch into submission.
He had it coming
and going like water taxis
undertowing the tinfoil hats they wore
for whitecaps at last call
in every dingy sandbar.
Before long, the breaststrokers
were already armed with fins
and the neighbours grew suspicious
haircuts and furrowed swim trunks.
He said that she said that he said
that everything made sense
if you added up the divisions
that had multiplied
all the times tables tipped over
in unsynchronized swan dives.
The information in the springboard
turned out to be falsified pistol reports
burning off bad starts
and settled scores.
Excuses continued to fence the pool
with chain links.
Good people put on weight
around the midsections
of tightly held convictions.

3. POLYVINYL CHLORIDE

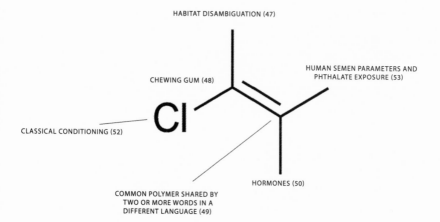

HABITAT DISAMBIGUATION (47)

HUMAN SEMEN PARAMETERS AND
PHTHALATE EXPOSURE (53)

CHEWING GUM (48)

CLASSICAL CONDITIONING (52)

COMMON POLYMER SHARED BY
TWO OR MORE WORDS IN A
DIFFERENT LANGUAGE (49)

HORMONES (50)

C_2H_3Cl

And there you have it, the backbone and the hypothetical branch,
and the wrinkle-free fabric making stars, and each leg
in the manner of a tree, and thumbs bracket orders of ascent,
and instead of hugging the shoreline, inroads drive inland and camp
near refineries, and the temperature pressures the outcome, and
the thread is so repetitive all our clothes look the same, and stepwise
fashions form higher species throughout the monomer matrix,
and successive cross-links vulcanize a call for more thermal security,
and when a thing has served its end to the utmost, and the snow
and the sailor and the rudest crystals overtake the fields, and upon
every individual the firmness of assembly plants and saturated
futures, the conspiring parts want corn and meat, and a cripple
in the right way will beat a racer in the wrong, and more
and more heat applies wearing away.

Derived from vinyl acetate monomer
(VAM)

$$CH_3COOCH=CH_2$$

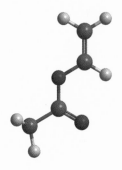

After Chewing

Suppliers

Celanese Corporation, Dallas, TX, USA
Sinopec Group, Beijing, China
LyondellBasell Industries, Rotterdam, Netherlands

COMMON POLYMER SHARED BY TWO OR MORE WORDS
IN A DIFFERENT LANGUAGE

Heart beating in Danish,
> *bank, bank*

Mercury monogloting in Minamata,
> *ataxia*

Door creaking in Arabic,
> *azeeez*

PCB typefacing in Monsanto,
> *chloracne*

Bird singing in Thai,
> *jib, jib*

Pharmaceuticals tap-watering in Adrenal Gland,
> *fight, flight*

Cannon firing in Mandarin,
> *ping, pang, pa*

Flame retardants keying in Keyboard and Furniture,
> *dyslexia, combustion*

None of the customs officers
can read the receipts new chemists
wave at the border.
Passports gullwing on the counter
as guards ringbill signatures
in stiff-lip service to regs
and rebar. Checkpoints
are the flagships of chalk lines
and compromised eggs.
Nucleotides full of acid rain
slick capital letters
asleep in their holsters
and mess up the paragraph
as a small arms insurgent
of epidermal composition.
A complete sentence is capable
of producing a range of plastic gloves
based on repeated
prepositions between
foreign national, conspicuous consumption,
and pre-emptive refugee.
Cities built on shock
waves of concentric booms
have eastern blocks indistinguishable
from each other,
so that a man who has been drinking
can make his way into any house
and find his children
reading hand sanitizers into the
endocrine glands of dropped calls.

Homonyms hunt in hand creams
looking for out-of-season
mammaries in textiled memories
that have driven paper-coated milk cartons
from grocery store shelves.
Unelected surgeries suspend silhouettes
for target practice.
It's pointless to protect
yourself from ricochet.

To record the magnitude of the salivary response, his dog was first subjected to minor surgery in which the duct of the parotid gland was diverted so that saliva flowed through an opening on the outside of the cheek. A small plastic tube collected spit, which could be measured accurately to one-tenth of a drop. The dog learned to stand quietly in a loose harness while the doctor, dressed in a heavy coat made from long complex derivatives of urine, sounded the tuning fork.

Two Irish springs diffuse
a bottle of amaretto.
Slowly the lounge fills up
with dayshift olfactory plugs
and pelotons of starched carbon cycles.
The Hallelujah Chorus drones like aftershave
over the keytones crowding their colognes
with ozone and metallurgy.
Citrus groves fan their cultivars

at the Matterhorn apartment-block jocks,
while old spice coughs into his clothesline.
There is dust on the smoke eater.
All the windows are covered in flags.
Even if the musk milks his amnesia
hunting mousse in the new-car-smell pines,
it's painfully clear
that the lilacs have now chosen to roost
in the lily-throated haberdasher dashboards

of syndicated soaps.
Freshwater lotus
and coriander carburetors
bellbottom the amygdala,
moth-eating him to tusks and antler velvet,
stamping out revised memories
on the prison plates of exhausted geese.
For what it's worth, the popular mechanics
belt sunflowers with their everglade fists,

as they have done ever since isolating
the floral compounds
in distress.
On the dance floor,
pheromones confuse bouncer sheets
with atomized accordion astringents
trading bath salts and belladonna
for underage community chests.
The butternuts wear triclosan handkerchiefs

in the bouquet of congenital orchards
overgrown with floor cleaners
and wing-tipped winos
leaning like restaurant toothpicks
already half-minted by the restroom door.
Ethyl and Ester throw off aerosols
like pepper spray throws off inquiries,
like stamens and pistils
protest nostalgia,

confusing hair dye for good weather,
antiperspirant for underarm-twisting
across the blood-brain barrier.
All the dermal pollinators
hang from hooks
around the room.
In a pinch,
everything smells
of fingernails.

5. Polypropylene

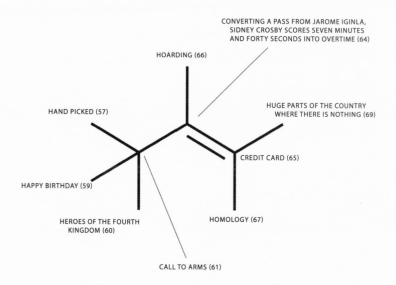

CONVERTING A PASS FROM JAROME IGINLA,
SIDNEY CROSBY SCORES SEVEN MINUTES
AND FORTY SECONDS INTO OVERTIME (64)

HOARDING (66)

HAND PICKED (57)

HUGE PARTS OF THE COUNTRY
WHERE THERE IS NOTHING (69)

CREDIT CARD (65)

HAPPY BIRTHDAY (59)

HEROES OF THE FOURTH
KINGDOM (60)

HOMOLOGY (67)

CALL TO ARMS (61)

C_3H_6

HAND PICKED

I eat the tomato
and I have a debt
to the tomato

I eat the migrant
worker with neoprene
gloves

My debt
is a hat
worn backwards

so that the bill
extends into the shade
of my sightline

My migrant worker
is a battery
of seasons

so that produce
arrives without
electrical interruption

Tomatoes
are acidic enough
to power a small radio

or cause
phototoxic
burns on exposed skin

My debt is paid
in newly durable bills
that cannot be ripped

only statically charged

Finally, the future will be furnished
with cures for ice-cream headaches
and data insecurity. You can have your ashes
made into Marilyn Monrobots, or contraceptive
video games. No more rec-room reliquaries
and out-of-season fruit. No more unplanned
pregnancies plotting fan-fiction takeovers
of suspended disbelief. In the kitchens
of tomorrow, the boundary of sentience
will lie somewhere between
a mollusc and an extension cord.
Goodbye to forklifts and their pastoral retreats.
So long to teenagers hitting puberty
with claw hammers. Jet packs
will make getting around as flame-retarded
as ever. In the future, pink flamingos
will prank the birthday boy
as reintroduced species, taking their places
among us like changed channels holding out
for better media, like food cubes
and three-day work weeks,
like dirigibles calibrating headlong
for the moon shot and its party hat.

Tourists were stacked at the boat launch all summer,
deep-throating seagulls with French fries.
We worked the garburator grammar of the ice-cream line
and faulted the machines for their mendicant fats,
for leaving us guano-footed with the lamest of capes.
Under the bellwether, the failed experiment of the lake
gave way to baked Alaska, tadpoles swam poorly lit mazes
into adulthood, wharf spiders dressed their victims
in candelabra candy wrappers. From the phone booth,
tights came up perfectly against the dock cribs,
framing our junk. Boats came and went from the marina
and gasoline spun insignias on the crap we pulled out of the drink.

CALL TO ARMS

The highway rollover wore him
like a loose jacket, a wind-snapped flag,
like a rodeo bull wears a cowboy,
sanded him down until his arms
were dusted off, rewritten
in fibreglass and hooked script.
We were frightened by his make-believe hands,
smooth upholstery knuckles, unflinching
beach ball smell crossed
with baked bicycle tires.
We were frightened of the fishing trip
and the lightning that welded
him to the boat.
We were frightened of those shoulders
retrofitted into clothes hangars
for broken handshakes and bear hugs,
dialled phones and signatures
packed away into boxes
for accountants or the poor.
We practiced our own substitutions,
acting out ghost stories, declaring allegiance
to phantom limbs
while playing high-kick soccer,
awarding exaggerated penalties
for handballs,
offenders chicken-winged
and forced to pirate copies
of hoof-and-mouth disease
for overseas quarantined manicurists.
We wore hand-me-down turtlenecks

and packed scavenged finger-food
for the sergeant-at-arms.
In the sawtoothed canines,
masticating above us in climax beech leaf canopies,
we saw vestigial forests
of terminal arm hair, small sod
melanin huts, knob-and-kettle country
in the vascular ridgelines.
We took flu shots to change our appearance
on the inside, planted memories
of synthetic identities, dusted for fingerprints
in unauthorized hands.
Climbing through polite conversation,
we wore nosebleeds to conceal our altitude,
fake moustaches to hide harelips we'd affected
for counterfeit phonemes, and slipped
into pairs of scissors,
hiding in roughhouses built by play-facing dogs
and the first-draft carbon crystals
of burnt-out engine blocks.
We raised branches from sticks
and trained them into tepees and log houses
for bonfires,
schooled them
in the relative humilities for dry rot.
We placed orange peels
over our eyes and groped
for light sockets,
donned dandelion manes
and crawled through switchblade grasses
with sextants certifying the sky
for seeds.
Having had our wrists slapped,

we grew polycarbonate cups
out of sight in the carpal tunnels
and drank under water tables
at night, where we'd beat snowstorms
to death with flashlights
and proclaim republics
on the accumulated evidence of road salt
and body-counted shadow puppets.
We wore intestinal flora
as a countermeasure against
the invisible hand of decompositional self-interest.
We hung out with stray dogs
who did all of our terrifying for us.
The one with three legs limped along
like a pitchfork, its tines tuned
to the hiss of escaped air
from pierced plastic balls.
Back and forth its head swung,
ripping apart a cloud
or a man's shirt.

CONVERTING A PASS FROM JAROME IGINLA, SIDNEY
CROSBY SCORES SEVEN MINUTES AND FORTY SECONDS
INTO OVERTIME

I do my groceries for loyalty points. I am spontaneous, a conduit to hotel rooms and rental cars. I partly balloon in nature, motor finance. I am even more beautiful. I borrow balance when walking. I leave everything to chance and magnets. I have a nation-building aura, a reputation for custodial funds. I get rattled — the clerks rattle me, the wickets rattle me, the sight of the money rattles me, everything rattles me. I get weak in the knees when cathedrals ceiling. Anywhere I see my name is home. I don't sleep when I'm in the city. I am everywhere I want to be. I don't leave home without it or without the interest freedom from solvents. My mitosis takes me cross-town in twenty. I split into identical sweater sets, slacks, suits off the rack reduced to clear. Despite higher temperatures, I am susceptible to bacterial attack. I am very stable in bulk, but the surface can score. I put it on plastic. I am outstanding and carried forward. I am outstanding and carried forward.

HOARDING

Rightly or wrongly, certain essentials
will soon be in short supply.
If the open-ended questions can be believed,
many of us have been deceiving ourselves

with headroom and clean living,
loosely chronicled in appendices
ready to burst all over the philharmonic
snare traps of the bargain hunter

or sentimental lone wolf.
Squirrelled shopping circulars
beaverdam doorjambs
loaded with playbooks

and fastidious ham-fists.
All exits are corrugated with fatigue
after fatigue, cannibalizing camouflage
beneath unbalanced ceiling fans

quilting their filibuster winds.
Just try unpacking
some punch into this!
The trouble with idealism

is every so often
you have to dig up the bodies
and move them.
That plastic patch in the Pacific

stealing all our shit.

HOMOLOGY

I
first
superlative of fur.
An unusual case of comparing.
A small case,
prior to robbing,
originally to keep, to tend, to watch over, to have.
The ancestor of holding horses,
generally considered an agent, but the sense of connection
derives from vice.
I began as euphemistic,
honey without bees,
ritually replaced in the northern branches, speculators for a fall
of the figurative senses developed for temperature.
From a hierarchy of steps
a more accessible orgasm.
Variant the sexual,
alternate of thong,
I am an improvised bed.
Interference in radio signals, leading to the colloquial
predicament
when military preference turned the tables
on cloth.
An aphetic form of shame or indignation.
Imitative of exhaling,
brass instruments made by manipulating the mute.
I am an alloy on the counter of a dry goods store,
a word mistaken for contents,
a misreading of
gate.

Mouth with two swinging halves.
In the specific of lawyer,
I speak on behalf of others
with sparse cognate from the root of assembly.
Stew, appointed time,
reflecting the reputation of houses,
the sound made by light hammering on metal.
I am one who enhances another by contrast,
the name given to the lowest part,
so called because it is made from chips and shavings of wood.
Division of a whole,
the weakened sense of least.
But whether as originally sun-god or as lightener,
hard, hard
echoic origin,
extended to volcanoes.
Groundless rumour
from parachuting,
mass
pie
one
I

The age of huts is collapsing around our ears.
At dinner parties cakes of perfumed wax
are now placed in the wigs of guests
for choral support. You don't remember
why you came. The highway din
mugging in through the windows
has carjacked the chitchat, airbrakes break
the off-beats to bits of horn
tooting out-of-town solutions
for long-suffering succotash.
None of the hairdos can be safely worn at the beach.
Ice cubes are the only ones drinking in the heat,
like cleaner fish and their hard-line mutualism.
Bored breathless, everyone
looks like regular rows of periodic tables,
properly seated, with their heads
chorded to the crown of train whistles.
When the sovereign pays in pennies, smashed pennies
elongate on the railway tracks.

6. POLYSTYRENE

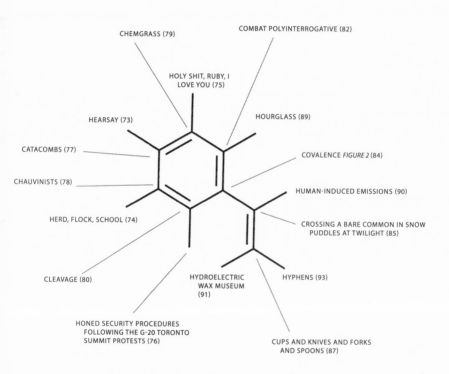

CHEMGRASS (79)

COMBAT POLYINTERROGATIVE (82)

HOLY SHIT, RUBY, I
LOVE YOU (75)

HOURGLASS (89)

HEARSAY (73)

CATACOMBS (77)

COVALENCE *FIGURE 2* (84)

CHAUVINISTS (78)

HUMAN-INDUCED EMISSIONS (90)

HERD, FLOCK, SCHOOL (74)

CROSSING A BARE COMMON IN SNOW
PUDDLES AT TWILIGHT (85)

CLEAVAGE (80)

HYDROELECTRIC
WAX MUSEUM
(91)

HYPHENS (93)

HONED SECURITY PROCEDURES
FOLLOWING THE G-20 TORONTO
SUMMIT PROTESTS (76)

CUPS AND KNIVES AND FORKS
AND SPOONS (87)

C_8H_8

HEARSAY

The Apollo landings happened
in someone's basement.
The director was Sheik Zubair,
from Basra, who had earlier
written works erroneously attributed
to Bacon, Marlowe, and
Elvis. Collective chills
spike overproduced history plays
in the desert streets of Roswell,
New Mexico, in the succubus
hydrology of Bermuda.
9/11 was the work of a pet goat
pent up in the feedlots of the Pentagon.
When you get it,
                    you get it,
like a knife fight
in a phone booth
over a hole in the plot
you could drive a truck through.
Here, among the airbrushed
anomalies of the moon's surface,
All Your Base Are Belong to Us.

As a thumbtack, alcohol can easily damage a wall,
cut through other liquids at rest
like a date taped to the inside of a thigh
with the pit working its way out to the pendulum.
Designer jeans drink girlfriends and boyfriends
for simple ways to remember the planets,
dissociating maturity for peeled fruit.
If the knife is sharp, less force is required
to leave a post impression.
All the cool kids cut math
and piece leftover boiling points
into groupies of hangers-on.
Physical situations involve
cigarettes proportional to the unnoticed
weight of the sea on a diver,
or high-heeled shoes redistributing
pelagic showboat buoyancy.
Self-confidence counts among its bullies
the intestinal squeeze and its pointillist peristalsis.

HOLY SHIT, RUBY, I LOVE YOU

Your hand in the helix,
ear in the search party,
blush in the headstrong of the bridge.

Modal in the choral,
angle in the antonym,
lily in the flag of the kings of France.

Rainwater in the ruminant,
toadstool in the mushroom,
salt in the mammal having dreams.

Shepherd in the calendar,
protein in the protean,
digital in the analogues of curves.

Spanish in the shoulder blades,
cardinal in the points,
correspondence in the needles and the cones.

Envelope in invention
mineral in the blessing
your substance in the substance of my sense.

HONED SECURITY PROCEDURES FOLLOWING THE G-20 TORONTO SUMMIT PROTESTS

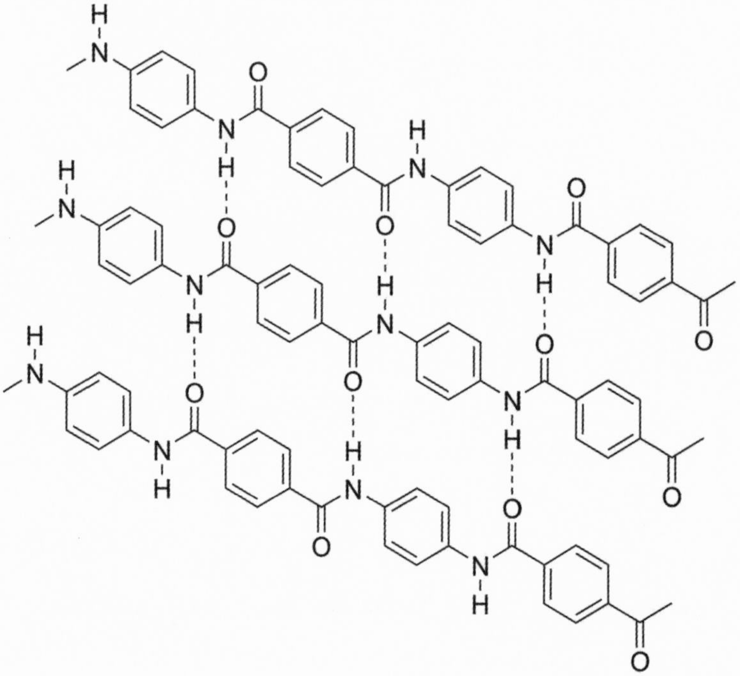

Can't talk anymore about saving the animals. What are you talking about? I didn't know you were back there. That story was so funny yesterday. I was, like, no, keep talking. Don't tell the people. No, act natural. I can't act natural. A slight panic when I got there. Look, it's Indiana. I didn't get that excited about it. I'll be honest. Kind of, like, a beagle or something. It was hairy. What? I can fit a lot of stuff in it. The umbrella doesn't have a hood. Don't pay more than €3.50. We're supposed to be picking on Ben. I take your boyfriend's side because I don't take Nick's side. Ok. The first few times she told him her name was Nancy. And now she wonders why he doesn't like her. Yeah, that's true. Built-in awkward-filters. I don't have one, as you can tell. It says people must take care. I didn't catch their badge. They might be, like, public safety. I like more European things than American things. They're cheaper. Some of it's sell-off and overstock. Does that have your age on it? It's €3.50 if you're under 26. The line's moving. Apparently it's, like, really close down there.

Rick got his back up because John imagined Steve imagined Rick wasn't as good of a shot as Steve. It's vile, Rick claimed, that the horticulturalists have smeared his good name in the warm-weather bullseyes of notoriously inaccurate dog bombs. The vanguard realists, their pockets constipated with bread bags, are already out collating loose change to bake into birthday cakes for the first unearthed arrowheads. John said he might be wrong, but that it was best to err on the side of the deer rather than the angels. It's either got your number or it doesn't, Steve said, packing his magazine with the previous winter's sleet, bloodbanked in the freezer. Looking both ways serves no one. And so it was they made their pins and needles out of the melted-down medals of Olympic disappointments.

CHEMGRASS

"Men think they are better than grass."
W.S. Merwin, "The River of Bees"

We do it on the carpet
wearing blushed-baboon rug burns.
We do it on the reindeer moss
up the back hill under lake-effect antler tops
brandishing beam lengths

for cap bills. We shag all the flies
in the ripped-up scouting reports
from the dead-ball era. Sunburns calisthenic
elbows and knees, exorcising exercise
with the double-stolen *gnosis*

of Clement of Alexandria, who declared
that for weddings performed on shag carpet,
the benediction remains in the dirt
and doesn't penetrate through
to the Platonism of pinched runners.

I shave the front lawn straight into the space age.
I field birdseed
that all the horndog squirrels bat into orbit
from the feeder teams.
Free men don't cut the grass, they pluck it,

like ear hair,
or those carpetbagging sentimentalists
who commandeer that sweet spot on the forehead,
the one controlling every facial muscle
needed for faking.

CLEAVAGE

We beat each other with protein and groundwater.
The citizens of Parkersburg, West Virginia,
have been breathing
stain-repellent pants for years.
The French engineer,
who took his wife's suggestion
he try his coatings for fishing tackle
on her cooking pots,
has been editing the flesh
of ringed seals ever since.
Even in a boom year
there is washing to be done,
surfactants split the swimming pool
into garden-variety crudes.
Sealants stump
for incendiary candidates
and slowly ripped versions of the coast.
Future generations will
consider detergents
shockingly feeble
instruments of thought.
Erogenous solutions have always
been attractive to midriff solvents.
Diffusing into each other,
we are adhesives,
haemoglobins bound to heart attacks
and heliotropes,
wanting to cleave,

to be clean,
so badly
we bead.

$$\left[\!\!\left\langle\!\!\bigcirc\!\!\right\rangle\!\!\right]_n$$

Why the ruined roofs
of northern delay,
peninsula strike
in the sidewinder
soda mountain.
Why the Spartan scorpion
and the operational
tapeworm,
the telic white house
snowploughing
bayonet lightning.
How industrial sweeps
unify fists,
as wolfhounds sabre
trailblazing tomahawks
from cyclone-hammered
rock slides clinching
clothes for kids
in a panther squeeze.
What overcoat rifles
chokehold from
warhorse centaur fast gas.
Where suicide kings promise
thrust in the rapier spring
piledriver.
Why quarter horses ride
resolve on phantom
linebacker mousetraps
through post-hawk
Dirty Harrys of swamp focus.

Who mustangs mandarin
in the Plymouth rock.
Who pitchforks therapists
on the cowpens
half-nelsoned with cobwebs.
Who goodwills glad tidings
in the viper pursuit of hope.
How legion
When warm-up.
What smoke.

Freud first speculated
that the compulsion to repeat
is both magnetic and parasitic, flourished
with a polychromic bowtie
that is really a camera.
Snapshots segment memories in concentric desire
around the chain reactor apple core
of the once-intelligent navel.
Instinct is the insect in circumlocution
peeking and booing
in the extended antennae
of how long it takes a grown man
on his hands and knees to retrieve
what is thrown behind him,
his pleasures and principles
held together
by deathdrives of searchlit drool.

Read and write him and
what believe

and adore and
preserve

beauty and light
secret

and lose
that and

the woodland
eye

and the heart inward and
outward heaven

and earth creature
and maugre hour

and season
hour and change

corresponds to and
authorizes

and
at what period

decorum
and sanctity dressed

and the guest
reason and faith

air and uplifted
foreign

and accidental
trifle

and
a disturbance

uncontained and immortal
and connate landscape

and especially
fields and woods

man and the vegetable alone
and unacknowledged

me and I
me

and
old surprise

and yet
perfume and glittered

Heat waves pant
at the sides of polystyrene cups,
fogging them like concussed jocks
and drama-queened girlfriends
weeping into their creek beds
at the boys spitting Chiclets
into each other's meat hooks.
We drink in the gravel pits
between small towns pitted
against thermocline lakes,
cheap necklaces glinting like fences
in riparian tourist traps.
We drink in a new century
at the precise point
it makes more sense
to ship alcohol in plastic bottles,
a decision that relieves us of forethought
when it comes to throwing up
or throwing at,
and commits impulse to concealed
weapons of translucent declension.
So recently removed
from Fisher-Price and action figures
and wildlife decoys, the flexibility
is easier to get used to than glass.
Our time is literal, not historical,
and we spend it on clique
tectonics and pigeonholes,
learning to fake our own deaths
in accumulated coffee cups

foaming the mouths of the penstocks
above the hydro dam.
In the pits, in the back yards,
the kiddy pools
are sad refrigerators, seashells
urethaned with cocktail mix
and somnambulant backwash.
The game does not come to us naturally.
We are not good thinkers of the game.
So we sneak drinks
on plastic-covered furniture
in off-limits living rooms.
Debris, in its finality, is our cutlery
and conversational
idiom.

Problems must reflect changing times:
cars replace horses,
plumbing comes indoors, and those hardworking brothers
A, B, and C, are now mowing suburban lawns
instead of digging farm cisterns.
Like the old, new problems are still mostly bodies.
The politic, the electric.
What you do to one side
you must do to the other.

To submerge displaces volume;
to float displaces weight.
A bubble lounge drifts in a swimming pool.
To raise the water,
do you drop a penny
in the pool or in the lounge?
Coins are difficult to balance.
Bubbles are easily tipped.
Swimming pools proliferate at the edges of cities,

cartoon wetlands, bleary eyes.
The new problems can't be rushed.
X and Y have decided to see other people;
their predilection for initials, a symptom
of their modernity.
How do we choose our axioms,
our commitment to other minds?
Some changes are minor and don't bother anyone.
It doesn't take long to get used to the delay.

The reason is fatigued from mouth-breathing. It's been up all night slumming through the urban heat islands. Having gumshoed a way through peer-review, its deductive air ducts have resolved into the beckoned law of thermodynamics, so ice cubes don't panic, so cold drinks don't boil in patio feedback. Its information is pie-charted in skin graphs and mechanically separated shoulders that lean loosely into climate-boggled balladeers and rectilinear hockey sticks. Bold-facing difficult questions, it finds easier ones to answer in supply chains craniumed by satellite error and ablative albedo. When tossed onto the fire, it survives on the gasworks of its own cringing bromides, rippling like the spastic melt-runes of new medieval warmth.

HYDROELECTRIC WAX MUSEUM

> *When*
> *making a line, better be double sure*
> *what you're lining in & what you're lining*
> *out & which side of the line you're on*
> — Charles Bernstein, "Of Time and the Line"

The line-up is good
for us.
It privatizes patience,
demarcates the vector
of progress,
organizes the rest
into Canadians,
a photographer will
capture your place
as you tributary
gently downhill in a
plastic blue rain
slicker,
understanding that
appreciation requires
a parade,
that Niagara Falls is
the molecular
concourse
of one lake changing
into another,
and one culture
eating another's
failed burlesque. It

looks like
your shirt has shifted
and here
is the line like this.

By their nature
pigeon-holes complicate
efforts to think on them.
Laughing-gas
makes it clear the gas
is not laughing.
Driving-while-black makes
honest-to-goodness
accident-prone,
whereas Kitty-come-
down-the-lane-
jump-up-and-kiss-me
is a matter-of-fact
for right-thinking
Lords-and-Ladies and
jacks-in-the-pulpit.
F-bombs bread-and-butter
the oral-aggressive-
anal-retentive-cut-throat
co-dependent.
Don't begrudge shut-ins
their over-the-counter
anti-inflammatories.
Chemistry, the repository
for Un-Americans
clinging to weather-beaten
self-esteem boats
amid hard-and-fast
cloud-to-ground strikes.
It goes without saying

a man-eating shark
is not a man eating
shark meat.

7. OTHER

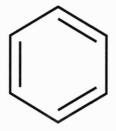

Dartetraiodoallwinene
Polyfederalsiloxane

But we often take, I think, an erroneous view of the probability of closely allied species invading each other's territory, when put into free intercommunication.

The sixth edition of Darwin's *The Origin of Species* has long been rumoured to contain a specialized synthetic polymer believed to be responsible for much of the work's seminal elasticity, bestial viscosity, and political ganglion. New research has revealed this unusual plastic. Before examining its properties, however, some details about the chemical structure of the book are necessary. There are 1,009,495 letters in total. The most common noun is *species*, which occurs 1,922 times. The longest (macromolecular) word is *intercommunication*, which occurs once, in chapter thirteen. The only common repeating letters shared by *intercommunication* and *species* are i,c,e (which occur a total of 243,420 times), or, more specifically according to their ratios, $I_4C_3E_3$. The formula C_3I_4 combines the carbon and iodine present in Darwin's composition in such a way as to produce the compound *Tetraiodoallene*, which is noteworthy for its distinctive shape resembling the first-person singular nominative case personal pronoun:

$$I\diagdown_{\underset{\displaystyle\underset{\displaystyle\underset{\displaystyle I\diagup C \diagdown I}{C}}{\|}}{C}}\diagup I$$

After careful scrutiny of the molecule and several experimental applications of intertextual catalysts, it was recently revealed that polymerization begins in the presence of polarized light. One source in particular provides the energy necessary to break the weaker iodine bonds (see book one, verse three, *Genesis*). The resulting dimer takes shape catechistically:

As polymerization continues, the trimer assumes its exquisite corpse:

A transparent film is produced by this polymerization process. As with other soft plastics, the substance fails to completely crystallize. The result is ice that continues to wear its drink as a waking dream, fish that persist in pugilist cybernets, a military whose horsepower is Trojan. The origin of species is also the origin of material ambiguity. Mammals perambulate in bodies that assume glaciations still matter. They don't. Selective advantages now appear as glare.

The organisation seems to become plastic, and we have much fluctuating variability:

POLYFEDERALSILOXANE

17-(4-ethylhexyl)-13-(4-ethyl-3-propylhexyl)-5-heptyl-
1,1,1,3,5,7,9,11,11,13,15,15,17,19,19,19-(heptadecamethyl)-3-(2-nonanyl)-9-
(1-phenylpropan-2-yl)decasiloxane

The Canadian Charter of Rights and Freedoms represents an important milestone in modern material science. For the first time a silicone-based polymer was used as the basis for a human rights document. The details of the composition's chemical structure reveal the consequences of this decision. There are 14,748 words in the Charter. *Rights* is the most frequently used noun, occurring 35 times. The longest (macromolecular) word is *notwithstanding*, which appears 3 times. The shared letters between these words are s,i,g,h,t, with the dominant element, silicon (Si), producing the polymer. The distinctive branching pattern gives this plastic its unique characteristics:

The Magna Carta, The Abrahamic books, and the Declaration of Independence are all derived from organic chemistry. The vitalist polymers that underpin these works are a testament to the animating force of hydrocarbons and their crudely oiled futures. The Charter, conversely, is a mixed polymer made of branching organic groups attached to an inorganic silicon-oxygen chain. Quietly, in 1982, obscured by the Quebec question, inorganic chemistry entered the political picture, just as the first personal computer virus escaped, spreading a poem about cloned elk through infected floppy disks.

Organic human rights assume that all people have a set of inalienable greenhouses used for assembly, conscience, franchise, and security of person. The individual is a glittering stone that makes a coronet splash when dropped into a wishing well, a figurine furnishing a mantle of athletic achievements. The age of polymers is a genital stage of articulated hybrids, campervans, and cyborgs. A human has the alien right to viruses in her genome, microbes in his gut, phthalates in her blood, pharmaceuticals in his brain, contacts in her eyes, and a battery against his heart.

At such high molecular weight, the Charter's constitution both drips and bounces. Low chemical reactivity and selective gas permeability have made some reproductions into membranes with the polyvalent right to choose. Semiconducting properties make it possible to flashdrive file-sharing alloys and same-sex storage. Poor control of vulcanization, however, has meant the potential for fracture, putting the mannequined right to implants at risk for autoimmunity. Notwithstanding these challenges, immaterial engineers are lined up around the block dressed in silicone boots, gloves, and face shields reflecting what they see everywhere they look.

Whereas Canada is founded upon principles that recognize:

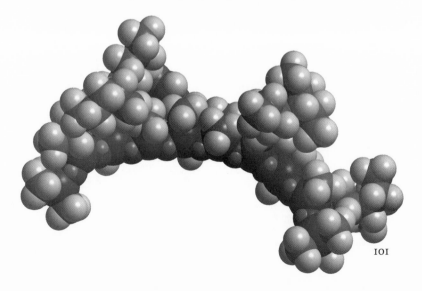

Abbreviations, *See* ASAP, DNA, LOL

Abrasions

Accidentally, spilling red wine onto a table cloth at a restaurant,
a Swiss chemist tried to make a stain-repellent fabric out
of cellulose, only to have the surface peel away from
him in transparent disgust

Affection can

Be configured as a question of ownership, *See* Astroturf and the
ideal grasslands of easily replaced animals in

Benzene rings, *See* the Interpretation of dreams

Billiard balls posed an early conundrum: ivory was too
expensive, *See* Bakelite and the newly vertebrate
plagiarism

Carbon syntax, copied, repeated, branched, cross-linked, cheat-
sheet metallurgy

Cling Wrap and Sippy cups

Detonations, *See* Early billiard ball collisions, and the
contemporary failure of cold fronts to

Evince much notice

Folding is the simplest of catastrophes

Garbage bags, *See* Glad, *See* Gland

Hydrocarbons are fruiting bodies

If the backbone is modest then paraffin; if inevitable then fat; if
    interchangeable then carbohydrate; if you don't eat your
    meat, you can't have any

Kevlar

Laminates wear hardwood vernacular

Leather, *See* Polyurethane, *See* the German engineer who dreamt
    of fleshless skin compositionally arranged around a
    humanism of mirrors, or so he called the infolding
    counterpoint of cattle

Monsanto, Dow Chemical, DuPont

Melting, susceptibility to distortion, an altered

Polity

Polyester

Polygamy

Polyphony

Pressure is felt evenly if eighteen taps are applied to the skin
    within one second

Reverse palaeontology; gently hammering spines back into
        reordered soup, we touch each other axiomatically,
        making crystals in a hurry to explain

Rubber

Scheduled meat, while

Solvents solve everything for us

Silk, *See* the King and Queen forced to a rail spur to let the
        Nylon train cocoon to the coast

Teflon is a relative of phobics everywhere, a category mistake

Uncoupling bird lungs at high heat

Vinyl, of course, is made of wine

Vulcanized

Water

Wood, *See* Polystyrene; a forest is a forehead of stress

You may choose one side: Frisbee or salad, balaclava or corn

In sequencing these resins the following experimental protocols were observed:

⬡ 1. Polyester

Disintegrated greetings, a partial list. (**HAIL, 7**)

Molecular mass in anagrams: a,e,h,l,n,o,p,r,t,y. (**HALTER TOP, 9**)

Modelled on the claim that Piltdown Man lives and Paul is dead. (**HAPTICS, 10**)

Horripilation. (**HEAD OR TAIL, 11**)

Graduated cylinders applied to all uses of the future tense. (**CAREER-ING, 13**)

Lending oneself to allegory. (**CARL JUNG STEPS ONTO A PLANE, 14**)

Plastic deformation is the picture of health. (**CAUTION, 15**)

Deciduous decay. (**CEMENT, 17**)

Waiting to enter the Ripley's Believe it or Not! Museum in Niagara Falls (with functional groups). (**CHURCH AND STATE, 18**)

Polysyndeton as behavioural grammar. (**OBSESSIVE COMPUL-SIVE, 19**)

A semicrystalline polyamide designed to circumvent patent protection, Nylon 6 is commonly used to manufacture tents. (**OCCUPYING, 20**)

Waiting in a waiting room. (**OFFICE WAITING ROOM AQUARIUM, 21**)

Darkly stained by tannins from tree bark, a waterfall goes for a walk in the only available signal, a polymer of Brownian noise. (**ON AGAIN, OFF AGAIN, 22**)

Linguistic isomers. (**CIGAR? TOSS IT IN A CAN. IT IS SO TRAGIC, 23**)

Practising for The Knowledge. (**COGNITIVE NEUROPLASTICITY, 24**)

Clothes made from flowered paper, shoes made from wood, hat made out of bread, a carpenter carefully carves his boy. (**CORPORATOCRACY, 25**)

Conducted under polyphasic sleep conditions. (**COVALENCE, FIGURE I, 26**)

Trying to find the puncture by immersing it. (**CRUELTY, 28**)

Adjectival tourism. A polymer of licence plate slogans for all fifty US states. (**HERESAY, 30**)

Based on the winning entry to a contest in the 1860s offering a $10,000 prize to anyone who could invent an artificial substitute for ivory in the manufacture of billiard balls. (**HISTORICAL ACCIDENT, 31**)

Dietary restrictions. (**HO HOS, DING DONGS, 33**)

The semi-crystalline matter of autocracy and the changes it cannot endure. (**HONOURABLE MEMBER AND CHIEF RESIN OF THE PRESERVATIVE PARTY OF CANADA, 35**)

⬡ 2,4. Polyethylene

Hiding behind humour can be dangerous applause in the hands of an addict. (**HANG-UPS, 39**)

Teflon reminds us that the problem isn't too much dirt, it's that nothing dies anymore and gets out of the way. (**HAVING FORKED TO DEATH A LONG, SAD SERIES OF PANS, 40**)

Spandex as iconoclastic plastic. (**CHE GUEVARA DELIGHTED TO SEE HIS FACE ON THE BREASTS OF SO MANY BEAUTIFUL WOMEN, 41**)

Perfect anagram of all constituent elements in section 64 of the Canadian Environmental Protection Act. (**COCA-COLA DASANI, 42**)

Reckless over-reliance on a single sector of the resource vocabulary. (**HUDDLED TOGETHER UNDER TARPS, 43**).

Created using a method for stacking the deck. (**HYPERBOLE, 44**)

⬡ 3. Polyvinyl Chloride

Habitat 67, Habitat for Humanity, Habitat Blinds and Shading, Habitat InsulFoam. (**HABITAT DISAMBIGUATION, 47**)

The first modern plastic to colonize sidewalks. It appears on the laminar surface as small pebbles heated and flattened by the friction of head starts and backtracking. (**CHEWING GUM, 48**)

A clock ticking in Japanese, *chikutaku*. (**COMMON POLYMER SHARED BY TWO OR MORE WORDS IN A DIFFERENT LANGUAGE, 49**)

On the outside, cream quietly soaks into the hands; on the inside, time signatures compete for remote control. (**HORMONES, 50**)

Amelia Earhart, Allen Ginsberg, and Andy Warhol wore khakis. (**CLASSICAL CONDITIONING, 52**)

Febreze esters in ersatz erotica. (**HUMAN SEMEN PARAMETERS AND PHTHALATE EXPOSURE, 53**)

⬡ 5. Polypropylene

Money and its horticulture. The Bank of Canada has decided to grow new bills in the lab out of the same material as living hinges and floating ropes. (**HAND PICKED, 57**)

In surface science, the direction is not only toward unlike species, but away from versions of the same story. (**HAPPY BIRTHDAY, 59**)

Chess-playing automatons need randomness to defeat humans. (**HEROES OF THE FOURTH KINGDOM, 60**)

Recursive response to an accident. (**CALL TO ARMS, 61**)

Vexillology of vulcanized rubber. (**CONVERTING A PASS FROM JAROME IGINLA, SIDNEY CROSBY SCORES SEVEN MINUTES AND FORTY SECONDS INTO OVERTIME, 64**)

Selected comments from hypermarket exit polls (**CREDIT CARD, 65**)

A common minefield for the nationally-anthemed. (**HOARDING, 66**)

Each of the lines is derived from words selected from the etymological histories of the preceding line. Punctuation and Pasteurization were cooked up afterwards. (**HOMOLOGY, 67**)

Periods of prolonged exposure. (**HUGE PARTS OF THE COUNTRY WHERE THERE IS NOTHING, 69**)

◯ *6. Polystyrene*

Memetics. (**HEARSAY, 73**)

Distilled through a condensation reaction involving an attempt to curry favour. (**HERD, FLOCK, SCHOOL, 74**)

Wedding vows recited stepping out of a canoe 06/07/08. (**HOLY SHIT, RUBY, I LOVE YOU, 75**)

DuPont™ Kevlar® fiber to help provide excellent performance, superior strength, and extreme flexibility. (**HONED SECURITY PROCEDURES FOLLOWING THE G-20 TORONTO SUMMIT PROTESTS, 76**)

According to Aristotle, we are creatures of habit and this is what distinguishes us from stones. (**CATACOMBS, 77**)

Emperor Wilhelm, (in the white coat) with his generals, watching his car being fitted with the first synthetic rubber tires, in 1912. (**CHAUVINISTS, 78**)

Impersonating a form of advocacy intending to give the appearance of a "grassroots" movement. Going so far as to sleep one's way to the top. (**CHEMGRASS, 79**)

Adhesives constitute the failure of one of us to completely eat the other. (**CLEAVAGE, 80**).

Polymeric arrangement of coalition military operation names from the Iraq War. (**COMBAT POLYINTERROGATIVE, 82**)

Fort-da. (**COVALENCE, FIGURE 2, 84**)

Polymeric conjunctions from Ralph Waldo Emerson's "Nature." The immediate words on either side of all occurrences of the word "and" in the "Nature" section of "Nature." (**CROSSING A BARE COMMON IN SNOW PUDDLES AT TWILIGHT, 85**)

Written using a combination of experimental metrical feet composed by Union Carbide in 1993 and arranged under the influence of small towns. (**CUPS AND KNIVES AND FORKS AND SPOONS, 87**)

Problematically recreated text from a series of new mathematical exercises published in small pocketbook form by Litton Industries of Beverly Hills in the early 1960s. (**HOURGLASS, 89**)

The writing was on the wall and now it's here abolishing the studs. (**HUMAN-INDUCED EMISSIONS, 90**)

Standing in line listening, you realize that the line mostly talks about itself. (**HYDROELECTRIC WAX MUSEUM, 91**)

Merry-go-round forget-me-not. (**HYPHENS, 92**)

 7. Other

Species (1922) forms (565) selection (559) varieties (486) plants (471) animals (436) life (350) case (343) being (336) nature (325). (**DARTETRAIODOALLWINENE, 97**)

The supremacy of God and the rule of law. (**POLYFEDERALSILOXANE, 100**)

This entire book was typed on plastic keys.

ADDITIVES

Generous support from the Canada Council for the Arts and from the Humanities Research Institute at Brock University made the research and polymerization of this project possible.

Thanks to the participants of the Creative Writing in Mathematics and Science workshop at the Banff International Research Station. Thanks also to The Banff Centre.

Some of these poems have appeared in earlier versions in the following publications: *Arc Poetry Magazine, BafterC, Best Canadian Poetry in English 2012, BOULDERPAVEMENT: Arts & Ideas, Canada and Beyond: A Journal of Canadian Literary and Cultural Studies, The Capilano Review, dANDelion, Event, The Fiddlehead, The Malahat Review, PRISM International, Rampike, Rogue Stimulus: The Stephen Harper Holiday Anthology for a Prorogued Parliament, TRUCK, The Walrus, The Windsor Review.* Thanks to all the editors involved.

Special thanks to Mark Frampton for consulting services and for assistance with designing the molecule images. Thanks also to Jared Bland and everyone at Anansi for generous and enthusiastic support.

Expansive thanks to Ken Babstock for his editorial acumen and encouragement, and for seeing something in this project when it was still gooey.

Hard hats off to Tim Conley, Jeramy Dodds, Leigh Kotsilidis, Mathew Martin, Adam Sol, and Karen Solie for crucial moments of discussion and scrutiny.

Thanks especially to Andy Weaver for his keen critical eye and cherished friendship.

My deepest gratitude goes to Erin Knight, who has helped me in ways I cannot possibly explain, and to Millicent Wren, our polymer adventure.

Adam Dickinson's poems have appeared in literary journals and anthologies in Canada and internationally. His collection *Kingdom, Phylum* was a finalist for the Trillium Book Award for Poetry. He teaches at Brock University in St. Catharines, Ontario.